2024 by Melissa Wingo
All rights reserved, including the right of reproduction in whole or in part in any form.
Drawn and designed in Sunny California.

MINIMALIST BIBLE VERSE COLORING BOOK

MELISSA WINGO

Coloring Tips:

- If using markers, there is an extra page provided to prevent bleed through, but you might need to add another page if there is still ink coming through.
- Use color guide on the back of the book for color suggestions.
- Colored pencils & crayons work great.
- Use 5-8 colors on each page to keep it simple.

Blank to prevent bleed through or just to Doodle

Blank to prevent bleed through or just to Doodle

Blank to prevent bleed through or just to Doodle ☺

Blank to prevent bleed through or just to Doodle

Blank to prevent bleed through or just to Doodle ☺

Blank to prevent bleed through or just to Doodle

Blank to prevent bleed through or just to Doodle

Blank to prevent bleed through or just to Doodle

Blank to prevent bleed through or just to Doodle

Blank to prevent bleed through or just to Doodle

Blank to prevent bleed through or just to Doodle

Blank to prevent bleed through or just to Doodle

Blank to prevent bleed through or just to Doodle ☺

Blank to prevent bleed through or just to Doodle

Blank to prevent bleed through or just to Doodle

Blank to prevent bleed through or just to Doodle

Blank to prevent bleed through or just to Doodle

Blank to prevent bleed through or just to Doodle ☺

Blank to prevent bleed through or just to Doodle

Blank to prevent bleed through or just to Doodle

Blank to prevent bleed through or just to Doodle

Blank to prevent bleed through or just to Doodle

Blank to prevent bleed through or just to Doodle ☺

Blank to prevent bleed through or just to Doodle

Blank to prevent bleed through or just to Doodle

Blank to prevent bleed through or just to Doodle

Blank to prevent bleed through or just to Doodle

Blank to prevent bleed through or just to Doodle ☺

Blank to prevent bleed through or just to Doodle

Blank to prevent bleed through or just to Doodle

Blank to prevent bleed through or just to Doodle

Blank to prevent bleed through or just to Doodle

I hope you enjoy this book.

My name is Melissa Wingo and I am an author/illustrator. I live in Sunny California with my husband and three kids. I love books, drawing, the Bible, gardening and running.

Thank you so much for buying this book! Please leave a review on Amazon. It is greatly appreciated!

Connect with me:
evelyn-fields@hotmail.com
IG @melissawingodraws
TikTok @melissawingo7
FB @melissawingo
YouTube @melissawingodraws

Free Printable Coloring Pages www.california-paws.com

Made in the USA
Monee, IL
01 May 2025

16669652R00079